L.A. NIXON
BRITISH RAIL IN COLOUR

First published in the United Kingdom in 1982 by
Jane's Publishing Company Limited
238 City Road, London EC1V 2PU

ISBN 0 7106 0224 3

Printed by
Toppan Printing Co (S) Pte Ltd
38 Liu Fang Road, Jurong, Singapore 2262

Cover illustrations

Front: class 86/3 No 86311 whisks an Anglo-Scottish express past
Greenholme towards Shap Summit on 16 April 1981.

Rear: a northbound class 254 HST catches the evening light as it
passes Doncaster motive power depot on 27 July 1981.

Right: three class 31/1 locomotives stand at the buffer stops at
Kings Cross on 7 November 1976.

INTRODUCTION

Almost 20 years have elapsed since diesel and electric traction ousted steam locomotives from the majority of British trains. Since those seemingly distant days many 'first generation' diesel locomotives have disappeared from the scene. Indeed few young enthusiasts today can recall the 'Baby Deltics', the 'Warships' or the 'Claytons'. More recent casualties, the 'Westerns' and the much lamented 'Deltics' became subjects of fanatical cult worship in the months leading up to their retirement. The unique qualities of these two types singled them out for special attention from their admirers, but future prospects for various examples of BR's ageing diesel locomotive fleet remain a hotly discussed topic when enthusiasts gather. Some types, like the English Electric class 40, appear doomed while the 'Peaks', or at least the eth-fitted 45/1 series, seem set to survive into the 1990s. The pace of change within BR's motive power fleet will no doubt be governed to some extent by the speed with which electrification plans are realised but progress continues relentlessly to reshape the character of the locomotives and trains which remain the focal point of enthusiast interest.

However, the discernible nature of the railway is not formed by motive power alone. Many other factors contribute to give the network an absorbing richness and these too undergo this process of constant change. The early and mid 1960s witnessed the closure of routes such as the Somerset and Dorset, which never succumbed to modern traction, while others like the former NER trans-Pennine Stainmore line were only conquered by the ubiquitous dmu. Happily the pace of closures slowed in the 1970s but the threat remains, as testified by the end of the electrified Woodhead route in 1981. Electrification, especially of the 25kV overhead variety, will without doubt continue to make its enormous visible impact, providing environmentalists with an enigma and railway photographers with an unwelcome set of problems. Changes in signalling and telecommunications have gathered momentum. In some cases this was a prerequisite of electrification but semaphore signalling has now disappeared from most BR trunk routes.

Trains too have changed. Steam heated, vacuum braked compartment stock and prestigious Pullmans have all but given way to air conditioning, eth and air brakes. Pre-nationalisation passenger vehicles left the scene long ago and parcels vehicles built to the designs of the Big Four were a threatened breed in the early 1980s. BR's freight traffic has undergone an enormous transformation and the process continues. The Freightliner has come to stay while the pick-up duty formed of loose-coupled four-wheeled wagons has virtually disappeared. Today's typical freight train conveys one commodity in vehicles specially designed for the purpose, often running at speeds unmatched by many passenger trains during the steam era.

One inevitable consequence of the process of adaptation by BR to constantly evolving commercial and national needs is increased uniformity and standardisation. HSTs appear at Aberdeen and at Penzance. Emu stock seen at Kings Cross looks very similar to contemporary vehicles in Glasgow. Resignalling schemes lead to the disappearance of signal boxes which once identified a line's earlier parentage. But this does not mean that today's railway lacks variety and interest for the informed observer. A means of transport which equally effectively can feed the blast furnaces at Llanwern or take the children to school on the Cambrian coast, can deliver grain to the Scottish distilleries or whisk the Tyneside businessman to the capital and back comfortably in a day still deserves attention and offers a wealth of fascination for anyone patient enough to seek it out. That the daily ritual of railway business is carried out unobtrusively in all seasons against a backdrop of Britain's magnificently varied scenery simply adds to the visual delights available to the enthusiast.

In this volume we can only begin to present a few aspects of this activity. A number of older pictures serve to remind the reader that it was not so long ago that green diesels pulled maroon carriages (and, on the former LSWR, maroon ones pulled green ones!), or that the hydraulics reigned supreme on the WR. But many of the more recent studies which form the greater part of the selection also bear evidence of the subtle and constant change in our railway system, a reminder that what we see today may be tomorrow's history.

The pictures represent a distillation of the work of several photographers to whom the publishers and I offer grateful thanks. Inevitably both film and format of the original transparencies are varied, ranging from rather faded 20-year old Agfa 35mm to present day Ektachrome 6 × 7cm slides. This accounts for slight variations in colour balance, grain structure and definition. The photographic styles embrace the traditional, the unusual and the *avant garde* in a mix which I hope is both appealing and stimulating. Except where indicated otherwise the photographs are the work of the compiler.

The illustrations are grouped around identifiable themes such as class of locomotive, geographical area, lineside feature or photographic theme but no claim of comprehensiveness is made: a clear reason, perhaps, for a companion complementary volume in the future.

L.A. Nixon
Hathersage

March 1982

Until 1981 Wath Yard was one of the three Eastern Region terminal points of the Woodhead trans-Pennine 1500V dc system. The surviving catenary can be seen on the horizon in this study of a pair of class 20s and a class 37 standing at the east end of the yard on 23 September 1981. Merry-go-round coal trains for Fiddlers Ferry power station which formerly used the Woodhead line were subsequently routed from Wath via Wakefield, Huddersfield and Standedge.

Pride of place in British Rail's fleet of diesel locomotives was until January 1982 taken by the class 55 Deltics. Introduced in 1961 to take the place of ageing Gresley, Thompson and Peppercorn Pacific steam locomotives they have, over the years, acquitted themselves well with many of the class covering mileages well in excess of 2,000,000. Their twin Napier engines each of 18 cylinders in an inverted triangular formation gave them a nominal power output of 3300hp, at the time the highest for a diesel locomotive on BR and sufficient to allow substantial trains to travel *up* Stoke Bank at 100mph for the first time. Distinctive in terms of shape, performance, smoke effects and certainly noise, these fine locomotives will be long remembered by enthusiasts since final examples of the class were withdrawn from traffic in January 1982. These two photographs depict scenes from opposing ends of their life spectrum.

Above: the prototype, the only main line diesel locomotive to run regularly on BR metals without a fleet number, wears her most attractive and distinctive striped pale blue livery as she hurries on an afternoon Leeds to Kings Cross express near Ordsall in July 1960. Note the white clad English Electric technician in the cab. *(Peter Hughes)*

Left: in the closing months of her BR service No 55015 *Tulyar* heads the featherweight 0933 Hull-Kings Cross semi-fast past Hatfield Colliery; a far cry from the halcyon days when she and her sisters were entrusted with working the crack East Coast expresses. *(David Nixon)*

Left: during the last months of their working life the class 55 Deltics, then allocated to York depot, were often diagrammed to work trans-Pennine trains to Liverpool, in particular the 0850 departure from York and its return working. Here an immaculate No 55002 *King's Own Yorkshire Light Infantry* finds seven coaches an easy proposition as she lifts the 1305 Liverpool-York up the 1 in 138 of the former LNWR route from Dewsbury to Morley tunnel on 20 October 1981. The train is seen passing Batley station. At one time the area to the left of the train was occupied by the station and extensive goods yard of the former Great Northern Railway.

Right: towards the end of 1981 the Deltics were much in demand for the haulage of enthusiasts' excursions. British Rail promoted the majority of these farewell tours in contrast to the corresponding last 'Western' excursions which were privately organised. The class 55s were to be found in the most unlikely places ranging from Oban in the west of Scotland to Bournemouth in the south. One excursion of note occurred on 2 August 1981 when the National Railway Museum's preserved Deltic *King's Own Yorkshire Light Infantry* worked a BR Merrymaker excursion from Newcastle to Middlesbrough and Whitby. In glorious summer weather No 55002 on the outward journey negotiates the industrial suburbs of Tees-side at North Ormesby. Note the motorised gate at the bottom left controlling pedestrian access to the level crossing.

Left: if the Deltics have assumed the limelight, then the class 20s continue to be the humble unsung main line heros of the BR fleet. Undoubtedly these sturdy 1000hp locomotives from English Electric have proved to be particularly successful, outliving all of the other former type 1 competitors from other manufacturers. The majority remained in stock in 1982 and many are likely to continue in traffic for some years to come. Their yeoman service has already been acknowledged by the National Railway Museum which has acquired the prototype No 20050 (formerly D8000) for preservation and eventual display.

In the scene opposite Nos 20126 and 20127 play out their familiar role as they head a lengthy train of empty loose-coupled wagons away from Tinsley South Junction, across the Sheffield & South Yorkshire Navigation Canal and into Tinsley Marshalling Yard on 21 September 1979. *(Trevor Dodgson)*

Right: for many years the class 20s, or 'Choppers' as they are now colloquially known, have found regular use during the summer months on holiday passenger trains from the East Midlands to East Coast resorts.

Here a rather grimy duo, Nos 20063/71, approach Barkston East Junction, near Grantham, with the 0824 Leicester-Skegness on 10 August 1981. *(David Nixon)*

Much of the former Midland main line in the early 1980s continued to be rather anachronistic in character. Apart from the newly electrified section south of Bedford much of the scene including stations, semaphore signals and sidings remained little changed from the days of steam. This was particularly so in the area around Wellingborough where class 45 'Peak' No 45117 is seen leaving with the 1509 St. Pancras-Nottingham semi-fast on 16 August 1980.

During the summer months the York-Scarborough line is host to a wide variety of motive power. On Spring Bank Holiday Monday, 25 May 1981, 'Peak' No 46023 ambles through typical English rural scenery between Kirkham Abbey and Howsham with a returning Newcastle-Scarborough excursion.

The class 37 Type 3 1750hp diesel-electrics, smaller versions of their class 40 sisters, have been another highly successful English Electric design. Built between 1960 and 1965 the class was multiplied to 308 examples and with the exception of the Southern Region they are found at work on most parts of the BR system.

Here a very dirty 37031 heads the empty Dewsbury-Earles Sidings cement hoppers under the aqueduct immediately to the east of the 3 miles 950 yards long Totley tunnel on 25 May 1978.

Until the direct line from Sheffield to Chesterfield (Tapton Junction) via Dronfield was opened on 1 February 1870, Midland Railway passengers from the south were obliged to travel via Staveley and Rotherham. The latter circuitous route, known locally as 'the old road' lost its passenger service on 5 July 1954. It still sees a heavy traffic of freight trains as few travel the heavily graded Dronfield route.

Here an unidentified class 37 passes Staveley with a northbound stone train on 20 September 1979. Just beyond the bridge can be seen a platform of the erstwhile Staveley station; beyond that is the branch leading to Barrow Hill motive power depot.

The BR/Sulzer Bo-Bo Type 2 diesel-electrics were being withdrawn from service in considerable numbers in the early 1980s and by 1982 it was rare to find this type working regular passenger diagrams. Until the spring of 1981 class 25 locomotives virtually monopolised the cross-country six-coach Crewe-Cardiff services, a task eminently appropriate to their limited 1250hp power output. *Left*: class 25 No 25042 approaches Ponthir with the 1510 Cardiff (Central)-Crewe on 14 March 1981.

Right: the progress of No 25126 southbound over the Settle & Carlisle line at Mallerstang on 15 April 1981 is reduced to almost walking pace as it struggles to keep its train of four-wheeled fitted vans on the move on the last pitch of the 1 in 100 climb to Ais Gill summit. Examples of this class continued to be regular performers on this trans-Pennine route at this period, although usually operating in tandem.

The twenty-two class 81 25kV electric locomotives were introduced in 1959 and although all are today nominally allocated to Glasgow (Shields Road) depot they are to be found at work on the whole of the West Coast electrified system. In the earlier years of their life they were regularly employed on class 1 passenger duties but, with the advent of the more modern class 86/2, 86/3 and 87 they have assumed a secondary role. However, here No 81010 gives southbound cars on the adjacent M6 motorway a run for their money as she emerges from the Lune Gorge at Low Gill and begins the descent of Grayrigg to Oxenholme with an up additional express on 4 May 1981. *(Peter Robinson)*

A location familiar to the many passengers of present day steam hauled excursions between Hellifield and Carnforth, Clapham, in the Yorkshire Dales was once an important junction of the Midland Railway. Prior to the opening of the Settle & Carlisle line in 1876 the line through Ingleton to Low Gill on the former LNW trunk route (the location of the picture opposite) was the Company's only access to Carlisle and Scotland. In this scene the link is still intact as green liveried class 25 No D7592 rounds the tight curve into Clapham Station with a Morecambe-Leeds train on 12 March 1966. *(Gavin Morrison)*

An unidentified class 86/2 takes a rooftop exit from Manchester Piccadilly and approaches Longsight motive power depot with an express for Euston. In the middle distance can be seen the electrification catenary of the 1500V dc Woodhead line which is still used to provide power for local emu services to Hadfield and Glossop.

In 1980, as part of the celebrations of the 150th Anniversary of the Rainhill trials, two 25kV electric locomotives, 86214 *Sanspareil* and 86235 *Novelty* (named after two of the participants in the 1830 event) were given distinctive liveries. Here *Sanspareil*, carrying a livery similar to the one now standard for classes 50 and 56, leaves Birmingham International at the head of the 1440 Euston-Wolverhampton on 24 June 1980. This comparatively new station, on the outskirts of Birmingham, was opened to provide easy rail access to the new National Exhibition Centre.

The early 1960s were halcyon days for the English Electric class 40s when they were entrusted with some of the top express duties on both the East and West Coast main lines. No D209, in the days before the introduction of yellow warning panels, heads a rake of Metro-Cammell Pullman stock forming the up Sheffield Pullman near Eaton Wood in July 1960. Note the vintage Pullman brake coupled next to the locomotive.

Metro-Cammell never built a modern brake Pullman and eventually these coaches were replaced by mundane BGs. In 1960 the prestige Sheffield-London service was routed via Worksop and Retford to Kings Cross whereas today all through expresses linking the two cities use the former Midland route. *(Peter Hughes)*

The only Pullman service to survive into the 1980s is the Manchester Pullman which serves the capital twice daily on weekdays. The livery of the Derby-built coaches, although distinctive, is simply a differing combination of the established BR blue and grey, and is a far cry from the stylish chocolate and cream of yesteryear.

Below: No 86021 hurries the afternoon up service past Basford Hall Junction south of Crewe on 1 June 1979, providing a reminder that as they are air-braked only, class 87 locomotives are precluded from working this vacuum-fitted train. Until 1966 the predecessor of this service was operated by Metro-Cammell 'Blue Pullman' multiple units but over the former Midland main line through Peak Forest and Derby to St. Pancras. The new route via Crewe was a distinct improvement for passengers who perhaps felt that the scenic delights of the Peak District were poor compensation for the extra 38 minutes required for the journey. (*Les Nixon*)

Above: subsequently the 'Blue Pullmans' were transferred to the Western Region to augment the WR sets before final withdrawal in 1973. In this scene a Paddington-South Wales train negotiates Sonning cutting in the summer of 1972. (*John Vaughan*)

On 29 June 1977 an unusual schools excursion ran from Dronfield in North Derbyshire to Hexham. While the passengers visited Hadrian's Wall at Housesteads the stock was stabled at Heaton carriage sidings. In this scene class 37 No 37095 at the head of the empty westbound train, skirts the River Tyne at Blaydon. With the exception of the daily Carlisle-Newcastle-Edinburgh return service, locomotive hauled passenger trains are today not a common sight on this trans-Pennine route. This is in direct contrast with events following the Penmanshiel tunnel disaster in 1979 when from 17 March to 19 August all East Coast trains between Newcastle and Edinburgh were diverted via Carlisle and Carstairs. *(Peter Robinson)*

Upon closure of the direct line from Dumfries to Stranraer on 14 June 1965 through services from the south to the Scottish port were routed via Kilmarnock and Ayr, adding considerably to the journey time. In 1981 one daytime return through Euston-Stranraer train operated during the summer months, the northbound service departing at 1015, the southbound at 1315. Class 47 No 47431 wends her leisurely way through the beautiful rolling landscape of Ayrshire near Pinwherry with the down train on 26 August 1981. *(David Nixon)*

At rest
Deltics Nos 55012 *Crepello*, 55003 *Meld* and 55021 *Argyll & Sutherland Highlander* at the now closed Kings Cross stabling point on 7 March 1976.

Class 50s Nos 50016 *Barham* and 50017 *Royal Oak* at the now closed Ranelagh Road stabling point, Paddington, on 22 July 1978.

Above: emphasising the rural setting of Carlisle Kingmoor depot, on a misty Sunday morning in August 1981 a line up of class 25s is headed by a solitary class 37.

Below: although only a sub-depot of Toton, Westhouses is host to upwards of twenty class 20 and class 56 locomotives over the weekend period. Nearest the camera in this scene on Sunday 26 July 1981 are (from left to right) 20164, 20162, 20173 and 20157.

The Western Region of BR and its predecessor, the Great Western Railway, have always been considered somewhat unique in character. The tradition was continued in the early years of dieselisation when a policy of introducing diesel-hydraulic motive power was vigorously pursued from 1955. First on the scene in January 1958 were the 2000hp 'Warship' locomotives of the D600 series powered by two NBL/MAN 12 cylinder L12V18/21B engines, followed in August by the first of the D800 series, with two MD650 engines.

Left: in this scene one of the latter batch, No D829 *Magpie* in its magnificent maroon livery, approaches Worting Junction with a down West of England express in July 1966. She was then almost half way through her working life; the locomotive was withdrawn from traffic on 26 August 1972. *(Peter Hughes)*

Right: the Western Region diesel hydraulic story concluded with the introduction in 1961 of the now famous 'Westerns'. Rated at 2750hp these fine locomotives were powered by two Maybach MD 655 engines. A rather grimy No D1049 *Western Monarch*, one of the batch built at Crewe in 1962, makes a fine sight in the later days of its life as it leaves Exeter St. Davids with a parcels train for Plymouth on 5 September 1975.

On 11 September 1981 class 56 No 56061 prepares to take a train of empty merry-go-round hoppers under the M1 motorway and on to the Bentinck Colliery branch at Pinxton on the Pye Bridge-Mansfield line. Regular passenger services over this line, which linked the Erewash Valley trunk route at Pye Bridge with Kirby-in-Ashfield (East), were withdrawn on 10 September 1951, although workmen's trains continued until 6 September 1965,

During 1980 it was announced that the class 56 diesel-electrics would also be outshopped in this new rather gaudy livery when No 56036 was selected to receive the colour scheme on an experimental basis. These locomotives spend much of their working life on block freight trains and in particular merry-go-round movements from collieries to power stations. Here, on the last day of 1981 No 56096, then almost brand new, moves a loaded mgr train south of Doncaster towards Black Carr Junction and prepares to take the line to Gainsborough.

Left: in the brief twilight period between the passing of steam and the extension of the West Coast main line electrification north of Crewe unnamed English Electric class 50 No 441 growls her way past Scout Green box on the last stages of the northbound 1 in 75 climb to Shap summit. At this time the famous banks of Beattock, Grayrigg and Shap continued to prove an obstacle to high speed West Coast Anglo-Scottish schedules, a problem solved in the short term by the costly expedient of operating principal trains with pairs of class 50s in multiple.

Right: an ambitious railtour organised on 22 September 1979 to Crewe Works Open Day proved tremendously popular and involved class 50 haulage from Plymouth. On a beautiful evening an immaculate 50008 *Thunderer* slogs her way up the long twelve mile southbound climb from Shrewsbury to the summit at Church Stretton on the return journey.

The narrow body (2.45m compared with the usual 2.82m of most dmus) of the class 203 diesel-electric multiple-units, built in 1958 especially to the restricted loading gauge requirements of the Hastings line, is clearly evident in this photograph of six-car set No 1037 rounding the curve towards Bo Peep tunnel and West St. Leonards on 27 April 1977. In May 1981 the buffet cars of these 6B sets were withdrawn and the five coach formations redesignated 5L. Note the compartment for the above-floor-mounted English Electric 4SRKT 500hp engine in the leading power car. *(Peter Robinson)*

One of the prestige trains of the Southern Railway was the 'Brighton Belle', introduced on 1 January 1933 when the electrification of the direct Victoria-Brighton line was completed. Three 5-car 5-BEL Pullman sets operated the service in pairs until their withdrawal in April 1972. In the final month of its life one of the sets, in their later distinctive blue livery, passes Wivelsfield with an enthusiasts' excursion. All fifteen cars have been preserved at locations as diverse as Stockport, Finsbury Park and Sheringham. (*John Vaughan*)

Left: one wonders whether the young passenger leaning out the leading coach of this 25kV class 304 emu is an enthusiast keenly scanning the line ahead for the next appearance of a class 87 on a down express. The train, the 1645 Stafford to Rugby local, was photographed approaching Whithouse Junction south of Stafford on 14 August 1981. (*Ted Talbot*)

Right: a 4-BEP class 410/2 emu dating from the late 1950s heads a London (Charing Cross)-Margate train out of one of the spectacular eastern portals of Shakespeare Cliff tunnel on the approach to Dover in August 1971. From Charing Cross many services for Ramsgate divide at Ashford, a portion taking the coastal route through Folkestone and the remainder the line via Canterbury

The former London & South Western main line from Waterloo-Bournemouth had the distinction of being the last on BR extensively to use steam locomotives for the haulage of express passenger trains. Electrification using the Southern Railway 660-750V dc third rail system, was completed in 1967. The 4-REP class 430 emus comprising two MSO (motor second open), a TRB (trailer buffet car) and TBFK (trailer brake first) were introduced for these services in 1967 and 1974. Set No 3001 heads a pair of 4-TC sets through Ashurst, forming an up service to Waterloo on the 9th August 1980. The train is about to cross the site of the former level crossing, at one time the cause of many a traffic jam for holiday makers heading for the New Forest and Bournemouth.

The electro-diesel locomotives provide some variety of motive power for enthusiasts living in the area served by the Southern Region. Operating on the 660-750V dc third rail system, the class 73s are restricted to a clearly defined sphere of operation since their 600hp English Electric model 4SRKT diesel engine is inadequate for high performance main line operation in non-electrified territory. In this scene No 73135 heads the 1734 Waterloo-Basingstoke service past Weybridge on 26 July 1979. *(John Vaughan)*

In 1982 it was expected that the 'Peak' 1Co-Co1 2500hp diesel electrics would be retained in BR service well into the final decade of this century. The class 45, and subsequently the class 46, were developments of the original ten 'Peak' locomotives introduced in 1959. Over the years they have given excellent service, particularly to the Midland Division, virtually monopolising passenger services from St. Pancras for more than twenty years. At the cessation of St. Pancras-Derby-Manchester (Central) services in 1968 a token through replacement service (on Sundays only) was offered taking trains via the Hope Valley. Undoubtedly the former route through Millers Dale was scenically more attractive but the moors of the Peak District National Park near Edale provide a magnificent backdrop for a class 45 working the 1855 up train from Manchester (Piccadilly) in August 1975.

North of Trent Junction on the Midland main line trains for South Yorkshire may either be routed via the Erewash Valley line or through Derby. In this study 'Peak' No 45137 approaches Alfreton tunnel and Alfreton & Mansfield Parkway station on the former route with the 1605 Nottingham-Glasgow (Central) on 16 August 1978. Note the trackbed of the abandoned slow lines to the left of the picture.

The 'Peak' diesel-electrics were among the first regular diesel performers over the Settle & Carlisle railway, taking over duties which often required steam locomotives to be double headed. The reign of the class 45s, albeit shared by the ubiquitous class 47s, continued into the 1980s, although the prestigious Scottish expresses from St. Pancras which they once hauled had been reduced to Nottingham-Glasgow semi-fasts. With the re-routing of even these services in May 1982 yet another small episode in the history of the Settle & Carlisle route was brought to a close.

Right: in glorious spring weather No 45056 tops the grade by the then recently closed Ais Gill signal box with the 1150 Glasgow (Central)-Nottingham on 15 April 1981.
Left: No 45036 picks up speed with the same train on the downgrade approach to Shotlock tunnel on 24 August 1981.

Right: class 25 No 25314 emerges from the spectacular western portal of Penmaenrhos tunnel near Colwyn Bay with the summer Saturdays only 0735 Nottingham-Llandudno holiday train on 15 August 1981. The LNWR obviously went to great expense to present as pleasing an aspect as possible to residents and holiday makers; the eastern portal, which is completely hidden from the public eye, is a very unprepossessing affair.

Left: in complete contrast is the northern portal of Great Rocks tunnel, one of the many bores constructed in the late 1860s by the former Midland Railway in their successful bid to link Derby directly with Manchester. The line between Matlock and Peak Forest Junction was abandoned by BR in 1968 but thanks to the efforts of the Peak Railway Society it seems possible that the route may be reopened, at least in part, in the future. In this scene English Electric class 40 No 40062 is working flat out on the surviving remnants beyond Peak Forest Junction as it powers a Tunstead Sidings-Northwich limestone train up the 1 in 90 to Peak Forest summit on 9 April 1981. Out of sight, but working equally hard, is a class 25 providing very necessary banking assistance. This particular class 40, formerly based in Scotland, is one of seven originally built with disc indicators and subsequently rebuilt with full panel ends at St. Rollox works.

The 101 class 35 1700hp diesel hydraulics, built by Beyer Peacock (Hymek) Ltd, were introduced in 1961 primarily for secondary and freight duties on the Western Region. They were, however, a short lived class, the final examples being withdrawn from service in 1973. In this scene No D7030, then only a few weeks old, leaves Newport with a Swansea-Paddington express *(Peter Hughes)*

For many years the English Electric class 37s have been synonymous with freight and mineral traffic in South Wales. It is rare for these locomotives to wander far from their home territory, a fact well known amongst the loco-spotting fraternity. Here, in the late afternoon of a sunny day in July 1980, a remarkably clean pair put their combined 3500hp to good use as they emerge from Newport Gaer tunnel with a Llanwern-Port Talbot train of iron ore empties. *(Derek Short)*

The peace and tranquility of the little station at Talybont is momentarily disturbed by a class 119 Gloucester dmu forming the 1507 (SX) Pwllheli-Dovey Junction on 7 July 1981. The length of the platform is barely adequate for a four-coach train. *(Stewart Jolly)*

The full-throated growl of class 47 No 47294 echoes round the slopes of Treffgarne Gorge as she nears journey's end with the 0926 Paddington-Fishguard Harbour on 25 August 1979. (*David Nixon*)

British Rail pioneered the concept of scheduled liner trains for the movement of freight. The first Freightliners appeared in November 1965 with the introduction of the London to Glasgow service. Since that time the system has developed to serve most major ports and industrial centres. In this 28 April 1979 study English Electric class 40 No 40155 eases a Manchester-Holyhead Freightliner out of Chester. The unique No 6 signal box, straddling the former Great Western lines out of the city, was to be demolished when a resignalling scheme was commissioned.

Holidaymakers returning from Scarborough to Scotland are treated to the dual delights of clean class 40 haulage, in the shape of No 40182, and the splendid Scottish scenery near Grantshouse on 29 July 1978. The train is about to pass one of the famous LNER lineside signs informing passengers that they are now 350 miles from London.

Class 26 No 26033 at the head of the 1145 Wick-Inverness, threads a particularly attractive section of the Far North line between Rogart and Lairg on 1 June 1981. Four and a half hours is the usual time for the 161 mile journey, an average speed of only 36 mph, but at least in summer it is a very pleasant scenic experience. Note the secondman about to throw out a package of newspapers for local residents. *(David Nixon)*

A train journey over the West Highland line is an experience not easily forgotten. The section between Bridge of Orchy and Crianlarich is particularly impressive with high mountains completely dwarfing man's intrusion. In this scene the 3524ft Ben Dorain and the 1330 up freight from Fort William with No 27204 in charge are picked out by the late afternoon sun on 9 April 1981. The train is approaching County March Summit (1024ft), two miles to the north of Tyndrum Upper station. *(David Nixon)*

In 1976 BR announced that steam operation would be occasionaly permitted over the line from Inverness to Kyle of Lochalsh. In the event this has not happened and the class 26 BRCW type 2 continues to reign supreme on this scenic Highland branch. On 30 May 1981 No 26043, working the 1108 Kyle-Inverness, suffered such a major power loss that no less than 110 minutes were required for the 14-mile climb from Strathcarron to Luib summit. Here she is seen struggling through Glen Carron at no more than walking pace, giving passengers plenty of time to savour some of the undoubted scenic delights of Ross & Cromarty. At Achnasheen sister locomotive No 26039 was attached as pilot for the remainder of the journey.

Crianlarich was once an interesting railway crossroads in the heart of the Highlands but following the closure of the old Caledonian route to Dunblane it is now no more than a junction of the lines from Oban and Fort William. In this scene No 27111 with the 0600 Glasgow (Queen Street)-Mallaig pauses in the shadow of snow covered Sron Gharbh on 11 April 1980. Note the SR van next to the engine and behind that the through Euston sleeper coach. The privately operated buffet facilities at Crianlarich are well known to regular passengers on the West Highland lines; unofficial lengthy halts are commonplace, reminiscent of 19th century practice before the introduction of restaurant cars.

More than 330 miles separate these two scenes of secondary railway services in rural Scotland. Georgemas Junction in the heart of Caithness is 147¼ miles by rail from Inverness and in consequence rarely visited by railway enthusiasts. In this scene, the 0615 from Inverness has divided; a class 26 can be seen coupled to the four coaches forming the Thurso train while No 26021 and a BG reverse to pick up the two-coach portion for Wick. A class 26 is able to cover one week's tour of duty on the Thurso branch and the return working from her home depot at Inverness on one tank of diesel fuel.

BRCW Type 2 No 27212, one of the class fitted with push and pull equipment for working the Glasgow-Edinburgh Inter-City service, heads the summer only 1343 Kilmarnock-Stranraer through superb scenery south of Barrhill on 27 August 1981. The train is traversing the section which was washed out in the floods of 27 July 1980 when earthworks were severely breached in two places, isolating a class 47 and her train for no less than three days.

A class 20 on rather an unusual duty at Newton-on-Ayr. No 20080 is in charge of the Ayr breakdown train which had been summoned to deal with a derailed oil tanker early in the morning of 26 August 1981. Extension of the 25kV system from Glasgow to the south west has long been mooted but in 1982 positive developments seemed unlikely. At present no fewer than thirty-three weekday return workings connect Glasgow with Ayr.

The North British Type 2 1000/1160hp diesel-electric locomotives, introduced in 1959, spent most of their working life north of the border. In this unique scene No D6137 pilots preserved North British 4-4-0 No 256 *Glen Douglas* into Spean Bridge station on the West Highland with 'The Jacobite' railtour on 1 June 1963. This Glasgow-Mallaig excursion was to have featured steam haulage throughout but the train locomotive, a J37 0-6-0, failed and was replaced by the diesel at Rannoch. *(Gavin Morrison)*

The grandiose single-span roof of the train shed at St. Pancras frames a Derby class 127 dmu leaving on a local service to Luton and Bedford on 6 May 1978. On the left 'Peak' No 45103 awaits departure with a Derby and Sheffield express while on the right an 08 shunts a train of empty vans. Modification of the track layout and the erection of the catenary for the impending suburban electrification has now, alas, totally changed this scene.

A pair of class 104/1 BRCW diesel multiple units stand at the buffer stops of the former London & North Western Railway station at Buxton in August 1980. From here the direct route to Manchester (Piccadilly) is notable for steep gradients and tight curves, coinciding with a tunnel between Dove Holes and Chapel-en-le-Frith. In consequence only the standard short bodied units of 17.53m length are permitted to work over the line. Freight traffic to Buxton is normally routed via the former Midland line through Chinley, Peak Forest and Ashwood Dale.

In Southern Region green livery 4-LAV electric multiple unit No 2949 catches the sun as it stands at the buffer stops at Brighton in March 1969. These four-car sets, built in 1932 for local and semi-fast services, comprised three non-corridor 2nd and one 2nd/1st corridor coach. (*John Vaughan*)

Contrasting shapes at Paddington. The exciting futuristic noses (or are they tails?) of two High Speed Trains are complemented by the angular Victorian station awning and by two functional galvanised steel buckets. Unsympathetic readers may enquire as to which is which! Note that the exhaust ports are not yet fitted with the deflectors which are now a standard feature of HSTs.

Class 47/4 No 47420 catches the late afternoon sun as she hurries the 1650 Liverpool-York express through Morley station on the former LNWR route on 27 August 1979.

Over the years the inter-city service linking Sheffield and Manchester has been the subject of change. Until 1970 the fastest trains were always operated on the electrified Woodhead route, augmented by an adequate loco-hauled, and latterly dmu, local service via the Hope Valley. When Woodhead was closed to passenger traffic in January 1970, many patrons considered the alternative dmu service operating from the Midland Station in Sheffield to be a retrograde step. A marginal improvement occurred in 1977 with the introduction of the distinctive Swindon-built class 124 Trans-Pennine and class 123 Inter City units. One of the latter is shown here on the final stages of the eastbound climb to Chinley North Junction on 15 September 1979.

The first moves to implement complete closure of the Woodhead line were made in the mid-seventies and not surprisingly it became much in demand by enthusiast tour organisers. Many special passenger trains traversed the line in the final three years of its life; among the last was the LCGB 'Christmas Tommy' railtour of 30 December 1980 seen here eastbound approaching Penistone with No 76006 in charge.

Yet another class with a chequered career was the 1200hp Type 2 (later class 29) Metropolitan-Vickers Co-Bo introduced in 1958. Altogether twenty locomotives were built for service on the London Midland Region, being delivered to Derby shed for working Midland main lines between St. Pancras and Manchester. Their unreliability led to them being modified by the makers, and by 1962 they had been banished to secondary duties in Furness, the whole class being allocated to Barrow shed. They were the only BR diesel-electric design to utilise both a four- and six-wheeled bogie.

In this rare May 1960 study, two 'Metrovicks' doublehead an up Manchester (Central)-St. Pancras train south of Chinley South Junction. This class only just outlived steam, the last were withdrawn in late 1968, although No D5705 went to Derby Railway Technical Centre for use on test trains. *(Peter Hughes)*

In recent times much has been written about the unique 1500V dc Woodhead line which linked the collieries of South Yorkshire with the power stations of Lancashire. Although preliminary electrification works were at an advanced stage at the outbreak of war in 1939, the final stage of the Manchester-Sheffield-Wath system was not commissioned until 20 September 1954. The line survived for only a further 27 years, the last service train passing westbound through Woodhead tunnel in the early hours of Saturday, 18 July 1981.

One of the line's 1868hp Bo+Bo locomotives No E26044 climbs the 1 in 124 between Thurlstone and Hazelhead with a westbound loose-coupled coal train on 11 November 1969. Note the superelevation of the track, clearly designed to cater for relatively high speed main line passenger traffic. Increasingly in later years the staple traffic of the line was merry-go-round coal trains bound for Fiddlers Ferry power station and in consequence a majority of the class were equipped with air brakes and a dual operation facility.

The former London & North Western line linking Lancashire with Yorkshire over Standedge is one of the more attractive trans Pennine routes. In its heyday no fewer than four tracks were required to deal with the traffic between Stalybridge and Huddersfield but the line was reduced to double track in the mid-1960s. Today the route is particularly busy again now that it carries additional traffic diverted from the closed Woodhead line. After a heavy snowfall class 47/4 No 47436 eases the 1005 Liverpool-York express through Marsden on 16 December 1981. Just visible beyond the rear of the train is the station, the reversal point for Leeds-Morley-Huddersfield-Marsden dmu services.

Overshadowed by the 1563ft Loose Hill, class 08 No 08749 takes yet another trip working of empty cement hoppers up the 1½ mile privately owned APCM branch from the BR main line at Hope to the former G.T. Earle cement factory at Bradwell on 16 February 1979. The 08, from Tinsley depot, was under contract hire to handle cement and coal traffic on the branch and returned to her home shed at weekly intervals for servicing.

For a few days each winter the scenery of the Hope Valley rivals that of the Swiss Alps. A 'Derby heavyweight' class 114 two-car dmu forming the 1223 local service from Sheffield (Midland) to New Mills grinds its way up the 1 in 100 towards Edale in February 1980. The lack of public transport to Edale and the popularity of the Peak District with hikers and ramblers from surrounding industrial areas are two of the reasons for the continued existence of this service.

The first BR 1Co-Co1 Type 4 diesel-electrics, introduced in 1959, had the distinction of carrying the numbers D1-D10 and the names of well known Pennine, Lakeland and Welsh mountains. The prototype locomotives (later class 44) were powered by a Sulzer 12 cylinder 12LDA28-A engine generating 2300hp but, proving none too reliable on demanding express passenger duties, were soon relegated to secondary passenger and freight diagrams. Subsequent locomotives, classified 45 and 46, were delivered with an intercooled version of the same engine uprated to 2500hp.

No 44004, bereft of her *Great Gable* nameplates, wheels a lengthy up mixed freight train past the site of York South shed and on to Holgate Junction on the East Coast Main Line in April 1978. (*John S. Whiteley*)

With the introduction of HSTs on most of the Kings Cross and some of the West of England express services the appearance of locomotive hauled trains on the former GN line from Leeds to Wakefield Westgate is becoming the exception rather than the rule.

Class 47 No 47545 emerges from Ardsley tunnel in the early evening sunshine with the 1730 Bradford-Kings Cross express on 28 July 1978,

Present day enthusiasts look back to the early years of dieselisation with particular interest. The pace at which the modernisation programme was promulgated brought, by today's standards, large numbers of brand new diesels of many classes on to BR metals in quite a short period of time. Some, including the Clayton Type 1s, later class 17, were less than successful and were doomed to a relatively short life span. Here a pair of class 17s, one in green (No D8524) and the other in blue livery, accelerate away from Kendal for Windermere with a lengthy parcels train on 26 July 1968. Note the two class 5 steam locomotives on trip workings from Carnforth, indicative of a period of relative prosperity; today the single line Windermere branch is host to nothing more than infrequent dmu service.

An immaculate 'Western' No D1001 *Western Pathfinder* stands outside Swindon Shed in April 1963. This locomotive was the first class 52 to receive the maroon livery later adopted as standard for the class. *(Peter Hughes)*

Class 50 No 50021 *Rodney* is momentarily bathed in bright sunshine as she heads an up express over Combe St. Stephens viaduct near Grampound Road on 22 May 1979. Of particular interest are the surviving masonry piers of the original Brunel timber viaduct which was superseded by the present structure on 11 July 1886. The first Cornish timber viaduct to be replaced (in 1871) was at Probus almost 2 miles to the west of Grampound Road station and 4 miles from this location. *(Trevor Dodgson)*

Although the English Electric class 50s spent much of their early working life hauling West Coast route expresses to Scotland they are associated by many with the Western Region and in particular with the West Country. There can be few who do not recognise the location of this magnificent scene. Brunel's famous Royal Albert Bridge at Saltash and its modern car-carrying partner provide a majestic backdrop for class 50 No 50036 *Victorious* heading west with a Liverpool-Penzance express on 5 April 1980. Today residential property obscures the view but no doubt the houses are keenly sought after by Plymouth area railway enthusiasts! *(Gavin Morrison)*

Few of the once numerous branch lines of the Southern and Greast Western Railways in Devon and Cornwall remain today. The picturesque 8¾ mile line from Liskeard to the coastal resort of Looe is a pleasant survivor boasting, in 1981, no fewer than eight weekday return workings. The branch is unique in that operation requires reversal of trains at Coombe Junction, a service particularly suited to operation by multiple unit. A three car formation, comprising a Pressed Steel class 121 single unit No 55026 and a Swindon class 120 dmu, Nos 51575 and 51584, leaves Looe as the 0839 service on 13 August 1977. *(Terry Flinders)*

A moment of intense activity at Tiverton Junction on 30 August 1962. On the left 0-4-2T No 1462 prepares to propel its single auto coach to Tiverton while at the up platform NBL Type 2 No D6335 is about to depart with a local for Taunton as 'Warship' D810 *Cockade* takes the through down road with a Liverpool-Plymouth express. *(Ken Plant)*

English Electric class 50 No 50020 *Revenge* wearing the latest livery of enhanced size for logo and numerals, wrap-round yellow warning panels and grey roof, heads a West of England express along the sea front at Dawlish on 9 October 1981. *(Derek Short)*

Bristol may be aptly described as the railway crossroads of the south west. In steam days it was here that LMS and Great Western locomotives were changed on through expresses between the Midlands, the north east and south west. Today it is usual for a single locomotive to work right through on those services which remain locomotive-hauled, as with this 'Peak' No 45036, leaving with the 1140 Newcastle-Paignton on 24 May 1980. Note class 50s Nos 50043 *Eagle* and 50044 *Exeter* in the background moving on to Bath Road shed.

The class 33 BRCW type 3 diesel-electrics were introduced in 1960 for freight and secondary passenger duties. These 1550hp locomotives are exclusively allocated to the Southern Region, being based at Eastleigh and Hither Green depots. All members of the class are dual braked (air and vacuum) and fitted with electric train heating equipment. The twenty class 33/1 variants were converted for push and pull working with emu and TC stock on the non-electrified Bournemouth-Weymouth line, while class 33/2 comprises a dozen locomotives built to the restricted Hastings line loading gauge. Here No 33044 gets to grips with the 1 in 60 of Parkstone Bank with a Poole-Liverpool express on 15 September 1979. *(Gavin Morrison)*

Despite the fact that the entire class had to be re-engined, the Brush class 31 A1A-A1A locomotives have acquitted themselves well since their introduction in 1957. Today they are synonymous with secondary duties on the Western and Eastern Regions. No 31403 eases a breakdown train southbound through the industrial suburbs of Leeds at Hunslet on 15 May 1980. This locomotive is one of a number of 31/4s which, while allocated to Finsbury Park depot, acquired a distinctive and rather attractive white waistband stripe reminiscent of the livery applied in the early years of their life. Additionally this is one of 24 locomotives which have been modified to provide steam or electric train heating along with a vacuum and air brake facility.

In a scene which has changed dramatically since the photograph was taken in April 1978, a 'Peak' rattles under the North Circular Road overbridge and past the semaphore signals of Brent Junction signal box, Cricklewood, with a Sheffield-St. Pancras express. Today overhead catenary, colour light signalling and emu servicing installations set the scene.

A similar fate has befallen the magnificent array of semaphore gantries at Aberdeen, one of the last complex examples at a major British railway centre. Class 40 No 40142, heading an express for Glasgow, is hard at work lifting her seven coaches up the 1 in 96 to Ferryhill on 14 April 1979.

If Barnsley and Wigan have been the butt of the jokes of generations of comedians such is the status of the humble dmu in the hierarchy of the motive power of British Rail. Although they are not the most comfortable of trains to travel in, ironically they can be particularly photogenic. Two- and three-car units so often conveniently and unobtrusively fit into rural and urban landscapes. Illustrated here are passenger services on two contrasting secondary routes.

Above: a class 105 two-car Cravens unit forming the 1747 Manchester (Victoria)-Oldham service traverses the single track remains of the former Lancashire & Yorkshire line from Rochdale to Oldham near Shaw on 20 August 1981. Both vehicles are power cars to provide an improved performance on the adverse gradients of this route. (*David Nixon*)

Left: a Derby-built class 108 two-car unit forming the 1118 Carlisle-Barrow in Furness on 31 August 1981, leaves the isolated but scenically located station of Nethertown on the Cumbrian coast. This is another line with a restricted loading gauge and only short-bodied dmus are permitted. (*David Nixon*)

Despite the density of HST operation into and out of Kings Cross station, class 31s continued in 1981 to haul empty stock workings through the tunnels and up Holloway Bank to the carriage sidings at Ferme Park and Bounds Green. On 18 July the crew of No 31181 patiently await the road with a rake of Mark 1s, while in the adjacent platform a railman tackles the 'insect squash' on the power car of a recently arrived class 254. (*Ken Harris*)

A superb panoramic view of the rail exits of west London at Westbourne Park. On 20 September 1981 preserved 9F 2-10-0 *Evening Star*, hauling a train load of enthusiasts bound for Old Oak Common diesel depot Open Day is paced by class 31/4 No 31413 at the head of a nine-coach empty stock working. Note the western exit of the LT Metropolitan line dive-under in the foreground. *(Peter Skelton)*

March is the major rail centre of the Fen country and is particularly busy now that most freight traffic has been diverted away from the East Coast route. The focal point is Whitemoor Yard which is still host to a number of regular wagon load freights to centres such as Wisbech. March motive power depot is just out of sight to the left of this picture of class 40 No 40192 continuing her journey south with an oil train on 23 April 1981. (David Nixon)

In December 1981 the government approved a £30 million electrification of the East Anglian main line to Norwich. On 14 September 1981 scenes such as this, depicting class 47/4 No 47576 leaving Ipswich with the 1231 Norwich-Liverpool Street were doomed to disappear for ever. *(Peter Robinson)*

The original concept of merry-go-round traffic? A pair of class 20s hauling a loaded northbound coal train is passed by a southbound coal haul in the hands of Toton-based 20183 and 20135 on 25 August 1978. Just north of this location at Pye Bridge is the Butterley branch, now operated by the Midland Railway Trust and the home of one of the two preserved class 44 prototype 'Peaks'. The abutments prominent to the left and right of the picture are the remains of a bridge which carried the Butterley Company's private line to their Codnor Park Ironworks.

No 56081, one of the Doncaster-built class 56 locomotives, takes a string of empty merry-go-round hoppers into the yard of Manvers Colliery on 10 September 1981. Visible in the background are the remains of the coking plant at Manvers which was taken out of service in 1980. As can be seen, the BR line from Wath Yard to the colliery bisects the plant and passes under the main Sheffield-Leeds main line which itself separates the pit from the carbonisation works.

D1013 *Western Ranger*, one of six class 52 diesel hydraulics saved from the cutter's torch, is run from time to time on the Severn Valley Railway. In this scene she heads, rather appropriately, a lengthy rake of preserved Great Western coaches near Eardington during enthusiasts' weekend, September 1981.

The North Yorkshire Moors Railway operating staff have also found it an asset to have one or two diesel locomotives in their motive power stud. During 1979 and early 1980 the prototype class 31 No D5500, on loan from the National Railway Museum, was in regular use along with their own preserved class 24/0 No D5032, formerly 24032. This latter engine, BR-built and powered by an 1160hp Sulzer engine, was one of a class of 50 and is one of three surviving examples. Here she heads a four-coach train at Ellerbeck and begins the descent to Goathland with a Pickering-Grosmont train in April 1980.

A Western Region Swansea-Paddington HST is seen from the footbridge leading to
Cardiff Canton diesel depot on 22 August 1979.

The area around Grindleford station at Padley belongs to the National Trust and boasts some of the finest scenery in the Peak District. Travellers on the 1630 Sheffield-New Mills local must have been particularly impressed by this sylvan scene as their two-car dmu emerged from the stygian gloom of the long Totley tunnel on 26 October 1977.

Fifteen years have transformed this scene of the Lune gorge south of Tebay, for today 25kV catenary and the M6 motorway dominate the view. On 29 December 1967 a class 40 heading a Euston-Glasgow (Central) express picks up water from Dillicar troughs to replenish the tank supplying the train heating boiler. Water troughs were once a common feature on British main lines and allowed steam locomotives to cover extended distances non-stop; today all have been removed although structural lineside features, such as those at Garsdale on the Settle & Carlisle line, often remain.